Spell Check:
1000 Most Misspelled Words

Like mispelled for misspelled. Like sacrilegious, fuchsia, inoculate, obbligato and 995 other trickies. Plus hundreds of deceptive proper nouns like Sikh, Sarajevo, Hanukkah, Beaulieu, Reykjavik and, yes, Piccadilly. And is 'i' always before 'e' except after 'c'? It's all inside. You need never be spellbound again.

The **One Hour Wordpower** *series*

WORD BANK
Expanding Your Vocabulary
WORD CHECK
Using Words Correctly
GOOD GRAMMAR IN ONE HOUR
THE NAME BOOK
THE SECRETS OF SPEED READING
GUIDE TO WORDPLAY AND WORD GAMES
CRISP CLEAR WRITING IN ONE HOUR
SPELL CHECK
1000 Most Misspelled Words

One Hour Wordpower

Spell Check
1000 Most Misspelled Words

GRAHAM KING

Mandarin
in association with
The Sunday Times

A Mandarin Paperback
SPELL CHECK

First published in Great Britain 1993
by Mandarin Paperbacks
an imprint of Reed Consumer Books Ltd
Michelin House, 81 Fulham Road, London SW3 6RB
and Auckland, Melbourne, Singapore and Toronto

A CIP catalogue record for this title
is available from the British Library
ISBN 0 7493 1525 3

Printed and bound in Great Britain
by Cox & Wyman Ltd, Reading, Berks

Contents

Acknowledgements

The ultimate authority for this book has been the *Oxford English Dictionary and Supplement*. Other works consulted include *Cassell's English Dictionary*, *Webster's New 20th Century Dictionary*, *Webster's Dictionary of Proper Names*.

The publishers are grateful to *The Times* and *The Sunday Times* for permission to reproduce extracts.

One in ten is a dunce at spelling

One in ten adults who took a simple spelling test for a survey failed to provide a single correct answer. Only one in six scored full marks.

One thousand people were asked by Gallup to spell necessary, accommodation, sincerely, business, separate and height. Women performed better than men, with more than 40 per cent scoring at least five compared with 30 per cent of the men. Only 27 per cent of those tested could spell accommodation.

The findings were disclosed yesterday at the launch in London of two video films aimed at improving spelling and grammar. Alan Wells, of the Adult Literacy and Basic Skills Unit, said the survey highlighted a "sad state of affairs" with more than four million adults estimated to be struggling to read and write.

Introduction

Perhaps there are people who are always one hundred per cent sure of their spelling, but you won't meet them often. More likely, they could be fooling themselves.

On the spur of the moment, how many of us can write down words like abrogate, afficionado, anomalousness, apophthegm and abysmal (Oops! One of those was misspelled) with the absolute assurance that they are all spelled correctly? Or the names of the famous Mogul temple at Agra in India, or the French national anthem, or the title of the Persian poem which contains the line, 'A jug of Wine, a Loaf of Bread – and Thou'? How about the President of Libya? Citizens of Monaco? Never mind that it's Magdalen College in Oxford and Magdalene College in Cambridge; the Colosseum in Rome and the Coliseum in London; a good many of us get stuck at Piccadilly and Marylebone!

Bad spelling isn't necessarily a sign of illiteracy or lack of intelligence; it's an indication that we're only part-way through the task of mastering the vast lexicon of words in the English language. A faulty memory, poor word or letter recognition, even basic human laziness can all contribute to standards of spelling ranging from the unreadable, inarticulate and sloppy to the occasional but embarrassing lapse.

The difficulty begins with the way in which written English handles the sounds of the language. We use around forty different sounds to express ourselves, yet have only twenty-six letters in our alphabet with which to write them down. This means that certain letter combinations have to double for different sounds, which enabled George Bernard Shaw to demonstrate that *fish* could be spelled as *ghoti*: *gh* as in *cough*, *o* as in *women* and *ti* as in *nation*.

It is also a fact that whatever it is, English has a word for it; so it is no surprise that against the Russian language with some 130,000 words and the French with around 150,000, the complete English dictionary will contain between 400,000 and half a million words. That's a lot to learn and remember, so you are excused the occasional slip-up.

We must also grapple with the problem that almost half the words we use are not English at all. From the Vikings on, we have begged, borrowed and stolen words (and have had a good many thrust upon us), few of which follow the rules of spelling, such as they are. All these rules seem to have inconvenient exceptions – the 'i' before 'e' except after 'c' rule is an instance of this. So the spelling of English is a real minefield, not rendered any less hazardous by the pernicious habit of modern commerce of introducing non-words like *pak*, *kool*, *kleen*, *arrid* and *squeez-ee*.

On the plus side, however, the English speller does not have to cope with funny little strokes, eyebrows and dots over the letters, nor with having to remember whether a word is masculine or feminine. Its rules, however complex they may seem, are child's play compared with many other languages.

English is a rich and bubbling brew, at the same time wild and disciplined, reinventing itself constantly, and capable, almost, of expressing the inexpressible. That is probably why, today, it is held in the highest esteem as an instrument of international communication, of learning, of creative vision. It is already the first language of 350 million people and the official language of a billion more. You can't beat it, so why not join it – and improving your spelling skills would make a good start.

One Thousand Most Misspelled Words

(Plus a sprinkling of real stinkers
and foreign words)

abate, abatable
abattoir
abbreviate
abdominal
aberration
abrogate
abscess, abscesses
abstemious
abyss, abysmal
accelerate, accelerator
accessory
acclimatize
accolade
accommodate, accommodation
accompanist
accrue
achievable, achievement
acknowledgement
acolyte
acoustic
acquaintance
acquiescence
acquire
acquittal, acquitted
acumen
acupuncture
addressee
adenoid

adieu [in Spanish, *adios*]
adjunct
admissibility
adolescence
ad nauseam
adulatory
advantageous
adventitious
aegis
aerial
aesthete, aesthetic
aficionado
a fortiori
ageing
agent provocateur
agglomeration
aggrandize
aggrieve
agribusiness
aide memoire
à la carte
alienation
alimentary
allege, alleging
alter ego
amanuensis, amanuenses (pl)
ambidextrous
amoeba
amortization
amphibious
anachronism
anaemia
anaesthetic, anaesthesia, anaesthetize
analytical
anathema
ancillary
androgynous
animadvert
annihilate, annihilation

annotate, annotator
annulment
anodyne
anomalous
anomie
anonymous, anonymously, anonymity
antecedent

If This Student Received a 'B' in GCSE English, Does it Make You Feel Like a Genius?

A few gems from the English paper of a 16-year-old that earned a B grade: cuircus, headake, bargin, libray, coushon (cushion), safaty, pationt, earlyst, simaler (similar), equaly, mearley (merely), appreachiate, familer, imeadiate, brouch, matiri (materially), cemitry, leasure, frerternali (fraternally), misalanios (miscellaneous) . . .

---

antediluvian
antenna
antipodean
aphrodisiac
apocalypse
apophthegm
apoplectic
apostasy

Majority of illterates live in Third World

From the newspaper *The Muslim on Sunday*

---

apostrophe
appal, appalled, appalling
apparel
apparently
appellant, appellate
appendectomy
appliqué
apposite
approbate
appurtenance
arbitrage, arbitrary
arboretum
archetypal
archipelago
areola [human tissue]; aureola [halo]
armadillos
armoire
arpeggio
arraign
arriviste
arrondissement
ascendancy
asphyxiate
asphalt
assassin, assassination
assuage
asthma, asthmatic
atelier
attenuate
aubergine
auxiliary
avocado
awesome

baccalaureate
bacchanalian
bacillus

'Ullo, 'Ullo! Wot's This 'Ere Then?

The following is a sampling of language misdemeanours committed in a London police station's crime reports. Articles reported stolen included a four birth tent, a Ford Cubrololey (Cabriolet), an Alpha Romeo, several garden gnombs and a carkey jacket. Offences were committed at Hybry (Highbury) Corner and Sidnum (Sydenham), and one suspect, who gained entry by forcing a skylark, was described as wearing a pale blue suite. Another was probably a Frenchman, as he was wearing a leather berry. Fair cop, guv?

baguette
bailiff
balalaika
balletomane
ballot, balloted, balloting
balustrade, banister
barbiturate
baroque
barrel, barrelled
bas-relief
bayonet, bayoneted
beatitude
belligerent
benefice, beneficence, beneficial
biannual (twice yearly); biennial (every two years)
bias, biased
bijou
bilingual
bilious
billet-doux
bimetallism
biopsy

bituminous
bivouac, bivouacking
blancmange
bogie (under-carriage); bogey (golf); bogy (ghostly)
bonhomie
bon vivant
bouillabaisse
boule
bourgeois, bourgeoisie
braggadocio

Twenty Most Misspelled Words

Early in 1992 *The Sunday Times* commissioned a leading UK examination board to test a sample of 1,500 secretaries, clerks, administrative and office trainees for ability to spell everyday words. Four words were misspelled by more than half the sample. Here are the full results, showing the percentage getting each word wrong:

Word	%	Word	%
practice/practise	54	competent	37
withhold	52	calendar	35
occurred	52	warranty	35
innovate	52	acquire	34
benefited	48	liaise	34
principal/principle	45	truly	34
incur	44	expedite	33
grievance	40	discrete/discreet	33
concede	40	affect/effect	32
transferred	39	accommodation	32

With the word pairs, the percentages are those who could not identify or spell the correct word in sentences such as, 'the principle/principal of the college visited the faculty'. Worse, 11% got 'secretary' wrong, and 7% could not spell 'train'.

bric-à-brac
broccoli
brougham
brusque
budgerigar
bulrush
bureaucracy, bureaucrat

cabriolet
cachet
caesarean
caffeine
caique
calendar (of days, weeks, months)
calibre
callisthenics
calypso
camaraderie
camellia
carburettor (carburetter also acceptable)
carcass
caress
carat (fineness of gold; weight of precious stones)
carpeted, carpeting
carte blanche
casualty
cataclysm
cataloguing
catarrh
catechism
cauliflower
caveat
centenary, centennial
cerebellum
cerebrum
chaise longue
champignon
chandelier
changeable, changeability

chargé d'affaires
charismatic
chauffeur
chauvinism
chiaroscuro
chiffonier
chihuahua
chinoiserie
chlorophyll
cholesterol
chromosome

Howlers

Poor spelling is not always a serious matter. Try
keeping a straight face through these student
howlers:
- Russians use the acrylic alphabet
- Daniel Defoe wrote simply and sometimes
  crudly
- At Nelson's funeral, fifty sailors carried the
  beer after laying in state on a catapult
- Paris was once haunted by many cortisones
- Thomas Gray wrote the *Alergy in a Country
  Churchyard*
- Before a caterpillar becomes a butterfly it is a
  syphilis
- Alfred Tennyson was England's famous poet
  lariat
- I enjoy being embossed in a good book

cicada
cirrhosis
clairvoyant, clairvoyance
clandestine
clarinet, clarinettist
cliché
18

climacteric
clique, cliquish
cloisonné
coalesce
cognoscente (plural is cognoscenti)
coleslaw
colitis
colloquial, colloquy
colonnade
coloratura
colossal, collosus
combated, combating, combative
commemorate
commensurate
commiserate
commissary
committed, committal
commodore
communiqué
complaisant
concomitant
concours d'élégance
concupiscent
condominium
confrère
connoisseur
connubial
consanguinity
conscientious
consensus
consummate
contemporaneous
continuum
contractual
contretemps
cordon bleu
cornucopia
coronary
corpuscle

correlate
corrigendum
coup (takeover); coupé (car)
crèche
crochet (knitting); crotchet (music)
croupier
cuisine
cul-de-sac
cystitis (bladder); cytitis (skin)

STRONG MEDICINE: The results of the office workers' spelling test do not astonish me. When my son started at his comprehensive school in 1972, I was told by the teachers of the English department that spelling was not taught because it did not matter.

A teacher at my daughter's primary school took a different view. He thought spelling did matter. Encountering "medycine", so spelled, in my daughter's work, he sternly amended it to "medecine".

This letter to *The Times* from a reader indicates that not all teachers, despite the best intentions, get it right!

dachshund
débâcle
début, débutante
deceased (dead, follows being diseased, or ill)
deciduous
décor, decorum
deleterious

delicatessen
delirium
demonstrable
deodorize, deodorizer
dependence, dependent, dependency
de rigueur
desiccate
détente
deter, deterring, deterrent
diabetes
diaphragm
diarrhoea
dichotomy
dilettante
dinghy
diphtheria
dismissible
dissimilar
dissociate
divertissement
domino, dominoes
double entendre (rarely double entente)
drachma
duodenum
dysentery

ebullient
ecclesiastical
echelon
ecstasy
eczema
edge, edging
effervescence
effloresce
effrontery
egalitarian
eighth
eisteddfod
electrolysis

elegiac
embryo, embryos
emolument
enamel, enamelled, enamelling
enfant terrible
enforceable
ensuing

Near Misses Even looking hard at some words it's difficult to tell whether the spelling is right. Try these; half are spelt correctly, and half are deliberate mistakes. Answers over page.

1. anihilate
2. lacquer
3. laryngitis
4. afficionado
5. resuscitate
6. surveillance
7. homeopathy
8. jewellry
9. liquorice
10. resplendent
11. umberella
12. chromosone

---

entrée
entrepreneur
envelop (to wrap); envelope (for letters)
epitome
equivocal
erroneous
estrangement
eulogize; eulogy
euthanasia
exaggerate, exaggeration
exculpate
exegesis
exhilarate, exhilaration
exhumation
expatriate
extirpate
extrasensory

facetious
facia (also fascia)
fahrenheit
fait accompli
fallacy, fallible, fallibility
faux pas
fiasco, fiascos
flamboyant
fledgeling
fluorescence
focus, focused, focusing
foetus
forbade, forbid
forbear (patience; also ancestor), forbearance
forebode, foreboding
forego, foregone (to go before); *see* forgo
foreman
forewarn
forfeit
forge, forging
forgo, forgone (to go without); *see* forego
fortieth
fortuitous
Fräulein
fuchsia
fugue
fulfil, fulfilled, fulfilling, fulfilment
fullness
fulsome
furore
fuselage
fusilier, fusillade

gallop, galloped, galloping, galloper
gargantuan
garnishee
garrulous
gaseous
gasoline (increasingly used over gasolene)

gastric, gastritis
gay, gaily, gaiety
gelatinous
gemmology
genius, geniuses (the plural is not genii!)
geriatric
germane
gerrymander
gesundheit
geyser
ghoul
gigolo

More on (or Moron) GCSE Grades

Asked to describe the landing of an aircraft, a young student was awarded a D grade in GCSE English for this effort: 'A preuer shape was apporching from the southern valley graerly they disitusis recililly design aeroplane cirlcing above'. Another student did rather better and was given a C grade: 'The machine touched down with prission in the rough mountqiness regane, with out even scraping its' serface'. Other candidates got C grades despite these minor transgressions: polosy (policy); amitter (amateur); ensiatic (enthusiastic); morage (mortgage); headech (headache) and carm (calm).

gladiolus, gladioli (plural)
glassful, glassfuls (plural)
glaucoma
glutinous
gnome, gnomic
gonorrhea
gouache
goulash
gourmet (appreciates food); gourmand (glutton)
grammar
grandeur
grandiloquent
gratuitous
grievance, grievous
groin
guarantee, guarantor
gubernatorial
guerrilla (warfare)
guillotine
gymkhana
gymnasium
gynaecology

habeas corpus
habitué
haemoglobin
haemorrhage, haemorrhoids
halcyon
handful, handfuls
hara-kiri
harangue
harass
hashish
hausfrau
hauteur
heinous
herbaceous
hereditary
hermaphrodite

herpes
heterogeneous, heterogeneity
heterosexual
hiatus
hiccup
hierarchy
hirsute
histamine
histrionic
hoeing
holocaust
hombre
homoeopath
homogenous, homogeneity
homo sapiens
honorarium, honorary, honorific
hors-d'oeuvre
humerus (arm bone)
hullabaloo
humour, humorous, humorist
hundredth
hyacinth

Enquire or Inquire: Enquiry or Inquiry?

Although, by a fine margin, the *Oxford English Dictionary* prefers INquire, it still remains a free choice. ENquire is the Old French and Middle English form, while INquire is the Latinized version. Caxton (inquyred), Spenser (inquere), Bacon and Tennyson plumped for the IN prefix, while Chaucer (enquyrid), Shakespeare and Milton preferred the EN style. Some draw the fine distinction between enquire (to ask a question) and inquire (to investigate). In America it is inquire, as it always is in *The Sunday Times*.

hydrangea
hyperbole (exaggeration); hyperbola (curve)
hypnosis
hypochondria
hypocrisy
hypotenuse
hypothesis, hypotheses (plural)
hysteria, hysterical

ichthyosaurus
idiosyncrasy
imminent (impending) – not to be confused with
    eminent (important) or immanent (inherent or
    permanent)
immeasurable
immense, immensely
immobile
immovable
impassable, impasse
impeccable
impresario
impressionism
imprimatur
impromptu
incandescent
incidentally
incisor
incognito
incumbent, incumbency
indefatigable
indefensible
independent, independence
indict, indictment
indigenous
indigestible
indispensable
indivisible
inexhaustible
inexpressible

infinitesimal
inflammation, inflammable, inflammatory
inflatable
ingenious (inventive); ingenuous (naive)
inherit, inheritance, inheritor
inimical
innocuous
innuendo
inoculate
inquire (*see* 'Enquire or Inquire', p. 26)
insolvent, insolvency
insouciant, insouciance
install, installation, instalment
insular
insure (to secure); ensure (to make certain)
insurrection
intelligent, intelligence, intelligible, intelligentsia
intercede
intermezzo
internecine
inter, interred, interment
interrogate, interrogation
interrupt, interrupter
intransigent
inveigle
irascible
iridescent
irreconcilable
irreparable
irrestible
irretrievable
irrevocable
isosceles
isotype
itinerant, itinerary

jamb
jardinière

Geometric change

From Mr Colin Dixon

Sir, Having just completed the marking of GCSE mathematics papers for a national examining group, I am fully convinced that the silly season is upon us once more. From the first 100 scripts marked the following spellings of a well-known triangle were gleaned:

Isocilies, isosoles, isosceleses, isoseles, iscoseles, iscoseles, iscocelles, isoceles, isosoclles, isoscles, isocoles, isoscoles, isocelesse, issocelles, isosales, isosalies, isosceles, icosolese, issoles, isosillies, issocelles, isoscellies, iscolesces, iscosles, iscoelise, iscocelleses, iscosoleses, iscolilis, ososellese.

On the assumption that words change by popular demand, then change is inevitable, but to which spelling?

Yours sincerely,
COLIN DIXON

Geometric change

From Mr Andrew Ashton

Sir, I read with interest the letter from Mr Colin Dixon (July 4) concerning the spelling of isosceles. He counted 29 different spellings in marking 100 examination scripts.

It reminded me of an excellent mnemonic, that would have been of use to his candidates. I learnt it in my school days at Newcastle Royal Grammar School and have used it ever since: 'I saw our Sherpas climb Everest last Easter Sunday'.

I wonder how many versions of the word 'parallel' Mr Dixon found.

Yours sincerely,
ANDREW ASHTON

From Mrs Anne Mathews

Sir, Mathematics pupils have to be taught the meaning of the word 'isoceles' before they can use it: if a teacher explains that 'iso' comes from 'isos', Greek for 'equal' and 'sceles' from 'skelos', Greek for 'leg', surely the pupils will have a better chance of remembering both meaning and spelling. They will also realise that there is both interest and practicality in knowing a little Greek.

Yours sincerely,
ANNE MATHEWS

jejune
jewel, jeweller, jewellery
jocose, jocund
jodhpur
joie de vivre
judgement (judgment in legal works)
juggernaut
juicy, juiciness
jurisprudence
juvenilia
juxtapose, juxtaposition

kaleidoscope
khaki
kleptomania
kohlrabi (the vegetable)

label, labelled, labelling
laboratory
laborious
labyrinth, labyrinthine
lackadaisical
lacquer
laissez faire
lama (Buddhist priest); llama (S. American animal)
languor, languorous
largess (although the French, largesse, is often used)
larrikin
laryngitis, larynx
lascivious
lassitude
lasso, lassoed, lassoing
laudable, laudatory
legitimize
leitmotiv (sometimes hyphenated: leit-motiv)
leprechaun
lèse-majesté
leukaemia
level, levelled, levelling

liaise, liaison
licence (a permit or authorization)
license (to permit or allow), licenser or licensor,
    licentiate
lieutenant
like, likeable
likely, likeliest
lineage (ancestry); linage (number of lines)
lingua franca
liquefy, liquefaction
liquorice
littérateur
locum-tenens
longevity
loquacious
louvre
lustre, lustrous

macabre
mackerel
mackintosh
maelstrom
maestro
maharajah
mahogany
maisonette
majolica
mal de mer
manage, manageable, management
manikin
mannequin
manoeuvre, manoeuvred, manoeuvrable
manqué
maraschino
mariage de convenance
marijuana
marriageable
marvel, marvelled, marvellous
masochism

massacre, massacred, massacring
massage, masseur, masseuse
matriarch, matriarchal
mayonnaise
menagerie
meretricious
meringue
metamorphosis

From Bad to Worse A large sample of
schoolchildren was given a spelling test in 1984,
which was repeated with a similar sample in 1989.
During the intervening five years, the percentage
increase of misspelled words rose markedly:

	1984	1989
bargain	14%	25%
library	14%	21%
merely	26%	39%
politician	33%	41%
exaggerate	43%	56%
committee	57%	75%
leisure	22%	33%
sufficient	29%	38%
appreciate	24%	30%
permanent	45%	51%

mezzanine
migraine
mileage (although milage is acceptable)
milieu
millennium, millennial
minuscule
mischievous
misfeasance
misogyny
misspelt (misspelled is a longer alternative)
mistakable

mnemonic
moccasin
model, modelled, modelling
monastery
moratorium
moustache
myopia
myxomatosis

nadir
narcissus, narcissi, narcissistic, narcissism
nascent
neophyte
nephritis
neuralgia
neurasthenia
niece
noblesse oblige
noisome
non sequitur
nouveau riche
nuptial

oasis, oases (plural)
obbligato
obdurate
obeisance
obfuscate
obnoxious
obsequious
obsolete, obsolescent, obsolescence
obstetrics, obstetrician
obstreperous
occur, occurred, occurrence, occurring
octogenarian
odyssey
oesophagus
offence, offensive
olympiad

omniscient, omniscience
omnivorous
onerous
opaque
opportunely
opportunity
opprobrium
orthopaedic
oscillate, oscillating, oscillatory, oscilloscope
osmosis
outré
overall
overrate; overreach; override; overrule; overrun

paean
page, paging, pagination
palaeontology
palate, palatable
palette
palliasse
panacea
panache
pancreas
pandemonium
papier-mâché
papyrus, papyri (plural)

High IQ Doesn't Mean Good Spelling

A recent study of 114 pupils at Strode sixth-form college in Surrey found that although their IQs were above average, their scores in spelling tests were below the standard expected of the average 16-year-old in 1977. Fewer than one in five could spell words such as erroneous, accommodate, allegiance, eligible and villainy. One in three misspelled the words foreign and initials.

paraffin
parallel, paralleled, parallelogram, parallax
paralyse, paralysis
paraphernalia
parenthesis, parentheses (plural)
pari-mutuel
paroxysm
parquet, parquetry
pass, passable
passé
pasteurise
pastiche
pâté de foie gras
pavilion
peccadillo, peccadilloes
pedal, pedalled, pedalling
pejorative
pelargonium
pencil, pencilled, pencilling
penicillin
peninsula
penitentiary
penny, penniless
perceive, perceiving, perceivable
peremptory
perennial
periphery
permissible
perorate, peroration
perquisite
personnel
perspicacious
phantasmagoria
pharmacopoeia
phenomenon, phenomena (plural)
phlebitis
phlegm
phonetic
phosphorescence

phosphorus (the element), phosphorous (the adjective)
phylloxera
physique
pibroch
picket, picketing
picnic, picnicked, picnicking, picnicker
pièce de résistance
pied-à-terre
pituitary
pity, pitied, pitiful, pitiable, pitiless
plateau, plateaux (plural)
playwright
plebeian
plethora
pneumatic
pneumonia
poliomyelitis
polythene, polyurethane
pomegranate
poseur
posthumous
potato, potatoes (plural)
preciosity
predecessor
predilection
prefer, preference, preferred, preferring
premiere
prescience
presentient
preventive
prima facie
primordial
principal (the chief)
principle (the code of conduct)
profit, profited, profiting, profiteer
promiscuous
promissory
pronounce, pronounceable, pronouncement,
    pronunciation

The Prevalence of Preventative

Why use preventative when the shorter preventive means exactly the same? Mr V Edwards, of Sittingbourne, Kent, admonishes users of the former with this little rhyme:

> Who coined the word preventative?
> Was there an incentative
> For someone so inventative?
> And could we hear of villains held
> In custody detentative?

propeller, propelled, propelling
prophecy (the forecast); prophesy (to forecast)
prophylactic, prophylaxis
proprietary
proselyte, proselytism, proselytize
prosthesis

Ptantalizing Ptongue Ptwisters

The English language abounds with words containing 'silent letters' (doubt, psalm, knot, sword, solemn, etc) but perhaps none so strange as the 'pt' words. Here are a few:

ptarmigan – a mostly white, grouse-like bird
pterodactyl – extinct featherless flying reptile
pterylology – the study of birds' feathers
ptilosis – a disorder of the eyelashes
ptisan – a barley water drink
Ptolemy – the Greek astronomer and
    mathematician
ptomaine poisoning – from eating putrefied food

protégé, protégée (feminine)
pseudonym
psoriasis
psychology; psychoanalysis; psychiatry; psychopathy;
    psychosomatic; psychotic
puerile
pulchritude
punctilious
purée
pusillanimity, pusillanimous
pyjamas (pajamas in the US)
pyrrhic

quadruped
quarrel, quarrelled, quarrelling, quarrelsome
quatrefoil
quay, quayside
questionnaire
queue
quietus
quixotic
quotient

rabbi, rabbis
racoon (raccoon in the US)
radius, radii (plural)
raison d'être
rancour, rancorous
ranunculus
rapprochement
rare, rarefy, rarefaction
rate, rateable, rating
rationale
recalcitrant
receivable
recherché
reciprocal
recognise, recognisable, recognisance
recommend, recommendation

recondite
reconnaissance, reconnoitre
recumbent
redundant
refer, referred, referring, reference, referendum
régime
rehabilitate
reiterate
rejuvenescence
reminiscence
remonstrate, remonstrator
renaissance
repellent
repertoire
replace, replaceable, replacement
reprehensible
reprieve
repudiate

The 'Bad Spelling' Syndrome

In the 1980s it was not uncommon for some parents, perhaps in despair, to wonder if there was a 'bad spelling' syndrome running in the family – the members of which (grandparents, parents, children) were intelligent but simply couldn't spell. Experts soon raced to the rescue with the theory that such people were sinistrocular (a tendency to use the left eye rather than the right) and were not taught to read phonetically but by 'look and say word sheet' methods – wonderful for the majority who are dextral (right-handed) and able to combine word recognition with reading. The left-handers, it is claimed, have difficulty with the word recognition method, retaining only a hazy recollection of the correct order of letters. The jury's still out on this one.

rescue, rescued, rescuing, rescuable
resplendent
restaurant, restaurateur
resurrection
resuscitate
retroactive
rheumatism
rhinoceros
rhododendron
rhubarb
ricochet, ricocheted, ricocheting
riposte
risqué
riveted, riveting
rotisserie
roughage

sabbatical
saccharin (the substance)
saccharine (sugary)
sacrilege, sacrilegious
sacrosanct
sagacious
salubrious
salutary
samurai
sanatorium (plural sanatoria or sanatoriums); often
    sanitarium in the US
sanctimonious
sanguine, sanguinary
sapphire
sarsaparilla
satellite
sauerkraut
savoir faire
schnapps
schooner
sciatica
scimitar

scintillate
sclerosis
scurrilous
scythe
seance
secateurs
secretary, secretariat, secretaire
seismic
seize
sepulchre, sepulchral
serendipity
shibboleth
shillelagh
siege
silhouette, silhouetted
sinecure
siphon, siphoning
sirocco
sizable
smorgasbord
sobriquet
soliloquy
somersault, somersaulting
sommelier
somnambulism
sophomore
soufflé
soupçon
sphagnum moss
spontaneous, spontaneously, spontaneity
staccato
stalactite (hanging); stalagmite (rising)
stationary (still, fixed); stationery (paper)
stiletto, stilettos (plural)
story (tale); storey (floor of building)
straight (line); strait (sea channel); strait-laced
strychnine
stupefy, stupefied, stupefying
subpoena, subpoenaed

subterranean
succinct
suffrage, suffragette
sulphanilamide
sumptuous
superannuation, superannuated
supercilious

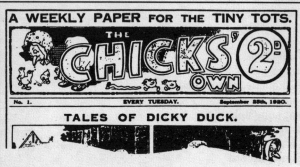

A WEEKLY PAPER FOR THE TINY TOTS.

THE CHICKS' OWN 2^D

No. 1.   EVERY TUESDAY.   September 25th, 1920.

TALES OF DICKY DUCK.

Ask Mum-my to buy 'Chicks' Own' ev-er-y Tues-day

When the children's comic paper *Chicks' Own* was launched in 1920 it became the world's first comic to be entirely printed in hyphenated syllables. It, and its later rivals, also became the vehicle by which hundreds of thousands of young children learned to read. A reader of *The Sunday Times*, Jennifer Gilbert, remembered how 'my mother's finger traced below the words and helped me assemble longer ones by building up the clearly separated syllables. As a result, I was an efficient reader when I went to school at four. The comic was an excellent example of the old-fashioned syllabic method of learning to read, and I owe my lifetime devotion to the printed word to it.' Reading was hy-phen-a-ted fun for ev-er-y one!

superintendent
supersede
suppository
suppress, suppression, suppressor
surrealism
surreptitious
surrogate
surveillance
sycophant, sycophancy
syllabub
syllabus, syllabuses (plural)
symmetry
synchronous
syncopate, syncopation
synonymous, synonymously
synopsis, synopses (plural)
synthesis, synthetic
syphilis
syringe, syringeing
syrup, syrupy

The Wurd Burglrs Ar At It Agen

Once a year, it seems, there is a fresh effort to
simplify spelling, and to introduce words like
'naw' (gnaw), 'dum' (dumb) and 'det' (debt).
Speling made eezy sounds like a good idea, but
so far every effort has finished on the junk pile.
Even the Simplifyd Speling Society (for that is
how they spell it) has difficulty getting its message
across. One of their press releases began,
'Aulmoest evrithing that we reed iz tiypskript at
sum staej . . .' Well, bak to the droring bord . . .

tableau, tableaux (plural)
table d'hôte
tachometer

tacit, tacitly
taciturn
taipan
tarantula
tattoo, tattooed, tattooing
telecommunications
temperance
tendentious
tepee
terrazzo
tête-à-tête
therapeutic
thesaurus
thief, thieves, thieving, theft
thyroid, thyroidectomy
timpani
titillate, titillation
toboggan, tobogganing
tomato, tomatoes (plural)
tonsillitis, tonsillectomy
toque (woman's hat); torque (rotational force)
tornado, tornadoes (plural)
torpedo, torpedoes (plural)
totalisator
touché
toupee
tourniquet
trauma, traumatic, traumatise
tranquil, tranquillity, tranquillise
triptych
trousseau, trousseaux (plural)
tuberculosis
tunnel, tunnelled, tunnelling
tyranny, tyrannical

ubiquitous, ubiquity
ultramarine
umbrella
unanimous, unanimously

unctuous
unguent
utility, utilitarian

vaccine, vaccination
vacillate, vacillation
vacuum
variegated, variegation
vehicle, vehicular
velodrome
vendetta
venereal
veranda
verbatim
verisimilitude
vermilion
verruca
veterinary, veterinarian

The ITA – Initial Teaching Alphabet

One of the most controversial methods of teaching spelling was introduced in the 1960s: the *Initial Teaching Alphabet*. Essentially but only approximately phonetic, it had a 45-letter alphabet which was described by one critic as 'a cross between upside-down Serbo-Croat and Greek'. Instruction in the nue speling went something like this: 'You can spell "fox" *focks* or *foks* but it doesn't matter because eventually we will tell you that it is really spelt "fox".' While it had its stout defenders among educators, others pronounced the results of ITA 'catastrophic'. Or, in ITA-ese, *kataestrofic*. Strange, but true.

vicarious
vicissitude

victuals, victualling, victualler
vinaigrette
vin ordinaire
vis-à-vis
viscous, viscosity
vituperate, vituperation
volcano, volcanoes (plural)
voluntary, volunteer
voluptuous, voluptuary

weather (climate); wether (sheep); whether (question)
werewolf
whereabouts
whereas
wherein
wherewithal
whitlow
whole, wholly
withhold
woe, woebegone, woeful, woefully
wool, woollen, woolly

yashmak
yoghourt, but increasingly, yoghurt
Yom Kippur

zeitgeist

I Before E Except After C. Who Sez?

Of all the rules of spelling, none is more capricious than the 'i' before 'e' except after 'c' rule, or, as the old jingle had it:

> I before E
> Except after C,
> Or when sounded as A,
> As in *neighbour* or *weigh*.

And of course most words do follow this rule:

- achieve, brief, fierce, niece, relieve, shield, shriek, thief and yield
- conceivable, deceive, perceive, receive
- beige, feint, freight, reign, rein, skein, veil

But, hold on! you shout. What about *either*? And *heifer*, *weird*, *sovereign* and *foreign*? It is true; these are all 'ei' words in which there is no 'c'. Nor is the 'ei' pronounced to sound like 'ay'.

To deal with some of these troublesome words, someone invented another rule: 'i' before 'e' except after 'c' and before 'g'. This effectively takes care of words like *foreign* and *sovereign*, and also of words like *sleight* and *height*, especially if you remember this addition to the original rhyme:

> I before E
> Except after C,
> Or when sounded like A,
> As in *neighbour* or *weigh*,
> Or when sounded like 'ite',
> As in *height* or *sleight*.

And everyone went home happy. Or did they? Because still lurking in the dictionary were such outlaws as *either*, *seize*, *seizure*, *weird* and *heifer*. To our knowledge they are still there, still untamed by any rule or guideline, except perhaps by that of the fondly remembered schoolmistress Miss Hall, who insisted her pupils learned the following:

> 'Neither leisured foreign neighbour seized the weird heights during the reign of the sovereign king who forfeited the reins of government. The heir feigned that the neigh of either reindeer was due to the weight, which was eighty skeins of yarn in the sleigh.'

Has Miss Hall collared the lot?

Rules to Retain, Remember, Refine or Reject

There are many more spelling rules besides Miss Hall's homilies; unfortunately many are so cumbersome as to be self-defeating:

> 'Words of more than one syllable, ending with a single consonant preceded by a single vowel, if accented on the last syllable usually double the final consonant before a suffix beginning with a vowel, as in commit/committing, excel/excelled, occur/occurrence, regret/regrettable.

Did you follow that? Could you remember it? Worse, there are some nasty exceptions to this rule: transfer/transferable and chagrin/chagrined, to name just two.

Nevertheless, here are a few fairly simple rules that may be found useful:

- Drop the silent 'e' when adding endings that begin with a vowel, like *able*, *ance*, *ed*, *er*, *ible*, *ing*, *or*, *ous* – as in love/lovable, persevere/perseverance, hope/hoped, write/writer, sense/sensible, come/coming, create/creator, grieve/grievous.

- Keep the silent 'e' when adding endings that begin with a consonant, like *ful*, *less*, *ly*, *ment*, *ness* – as in care/careful, tire/tireless, love/lovely, move/movement, like/likeness. Unfortunately you must also remember the few exceptions to this rule: argue/argument, due/duly, true/truly and whole/wholly. You can make your own judgement/judgment on judge.

- Keep the silent 'e' when adding the endings *able* and *ous* to words that end in *ce* or *ge*, as in notice/

49

noticeable, marriage/marriageable, advantage/
advantageous.

- Words that end in 'l' keep it when adding *ly*, as in
  cool/coolly, local/locally, poetical/poetically.

- With words ending in 'c', add a 'k' before endings
  like *ed*, *ing*, and *y*, as in mimic/mimicked/
  mimicking, panic/panicky, traffic/trafficking, frolic/
  frolicking.

- With words ending in 'n' keep the 'n' when adding
  ness, as in clean/cleanness, thin/thinness, sudden/
  suddenness.

- When a word ends in *ee* or *oo*, keep the letter pairs
  whatever you are adding, as in see/seeing, glee/
  gleeful, woo/wooed/wooing.

There is obviously a limit to the number of such rules
that the average speller can absorb, remember and
apply quickly when required. For most of us,
unfortunately, spelling consists of two choices: learning
the hard way, or, as Mark Twain put it, 'I don't give
a damn for a man that can spell a word only one way.'

Word Imperfect

Hemingway Jones was a brilliant novelist, yet no publisher had yet accepted his work. The trouble was, Hemingway couldn't spell. If only he had someone to correct his spelling, he'd be a famous writer in no time! So why not help him? Here are the opening paragraphs of his new novel, *The Biege Bhudda of Bagdhad*:

The old vetrinarian paused under the verandah, perspiring in his kakhi jacket. It was at least ninety farenheit. Mosquitos wirred over his head and, crouching under the fuchsia, an iguano flickered its evil tongue at him, iridescent in the flourescent glow of the parrafin lamp.

It had been a long day. First, he'd vacillated Mrs Horner's chihwahwa for diptheria and pneumonia. The poor animal had squirmed and writhed so much that the needle had perpetrated Mrs Horner's prosterior instead; now he could look forward with certainety to a lawsuite. Then there was that hysterical hippopotomus with a predeliction for *homeo sapiens*. And, finally, the marahraja's pink parrakeet with the swollen proboscis and a fine vocabluary of words not suitable for the ears of young ladies.

The vet sank wearily down on the chaise longue near the rhododendhrons, poured himself a generous shot of Irish whisky, and considered his dilemna. Would he continue here and risk a coronory, or take up the more congenial post at the armadillo park in the Carribean?

[Answers over page]

Problem Proper Nouns

For every word we use in the course of an average day, we probably use five times as many proper nouns or names. Many of these are commonly misspelled, too, so here is a short list of those likely to cause trouble. The names of people – surnames and given names – are covered in another volume in the **One Hour Wordpower** series, *The Name Book*.

Abergavenny, Gwent, Wales
Aberystwyth, Dyfed, Wales
Abyssinia
Aldeburgh, Suffolk
Appelation Controlée
Archimedes
Achilles tendon
Aer Lingus
Afghanistan

Answers to Word Imperfect

If Hemingway Jones used the following spellings, his novel might stand a better chance: beige/buddha/Baghdad/veterinarian/veranda/ khaki/fahrenheit/ Mosquitoes/whirred/iguana/ fluorescent/paraffin/vaccinated/ chihuahua/ diphtheria/penetrated/posterior/certainty/lawsuit/ hippopotamus/predilection/*homo sapiens*/ maharajah's/ parakeet/vocabulary/ rhododendrons/dilemma/coronary/Caribbean. Twenty correct is a reasonable score. There is no such thing as Irish whisky, by the way; whisky is exclusive to Scotland. It should be Irish whiskey.

Agamemnon
Aladdin
Aldwych
Algonquin Hotel, New York
Alsace-Lorraine
Alzheimer's disease
Amontillado sherry
Annunciation
Anorexia nervosa
Apache
Aphrodite
Apocalypse
Appalachia
Arbroath, Tayside
Arc de Triomphe
Aristotle
Armageddon
Art nouveau
Ascension Day
Ashby-de-la-Zouch, Leicestershire
Athanaeum Club
Aubusson carpets
Audubon Society
Augean stables
Auld Lang Syne
Auld Reekie
Aurora Borealis
Auschwitz
Axminster carpets
Azerbaijan

Babylon
Baccalauréat
Bacchus
Baedeker (travel guides)
Baghdad
Baha'i (faith)
Bahrain

Balthazar
Bannockburn
Barabbas
Bathsheba
Bayreuth Festival
Béarnaise sauce
Beau Brummell
Beaufort scale
Beau Geste
Beaujolais
Beaulieu Castle, Hampshire
Bechuanaland
Beelzebub
Belshazzar's Feast
Berchtesgaden
Betws-y-Coed
Bishop's Stortford
Blenheim Palace, Oxfordshire
Bletchley
Boadicea
Bohème, La (opera)
Bohemian
Bokhara rugs
Bordeaux
Boris Godunov (opera)
Boughton Monchelsea
Bouillabaisse
Bourgogne, France
Bovey Tracey, Devon
Braille
Brechtian
Brightlingsea, Essex
Britannia
Brittany
Brummagem
Buchenwald
Buddha
Bundestag

The Ligature Untied

Caesar, manoeuvre, aesthetic, oenology, mediaeval, encyclopaedia and archaeology are words that once contained a ligature, either a joined ae (æ) or a joined oe (œ). The trend today is to separate them – very few typewriters and computer keyboards accommodate ligatures, anyway – and to further simplify the word by squeezing out one of the letters, resulting in esthetic, medieval, maneuver, primeval, and so on. This process is rather more advanced in America than it is in Britain.

Caernarfon (not Carnarvon), Gwynedd
Caerphilly, Glamorgan
Caesar, Caesarian
Camembert
Cape Canaveral
Capodimonte porcelain
Caribbean
Casablanca
Casbah
Cerebral thrombosis
Cerne Abbas, Dorset
Chapel-en-le-Frith, Derbyshire
Chardonnay
Charlemagne
Chartreuse
Chateaubriand
Château d'Yquem
Cheyenne
Chianti
Cincinnati
Cinque Ports
Cirencester, Gloucestershire
Coq au vin

Coquilles St Jacques
Coliseum (London)
Colosseum (Rome)
Comanche
Comédie-Français
Comédie humaine
Compton Wynyates, Warwickshire
Connecticut
Cosa Nostra
Così fan tutte
Courtauld Institute
Crème brûlée
Crêpe suzette
Criccieth, Gwynedd
Curaçao
Czechoslovakia

Dadaism
Daguerrotype
Dail Eirann (Republic of Ireland parliament)
Daiquiri
Dalai Lama
Daphnis and Chloe
Dardanelles
Darjeeling
Déjà vu
Déjeuner sur l'herbe (Manet's painting)
Delhi
Demoiselles d'Avignon (Picasso's painting)
Deuteronomy
Deutschland
Diaspora, The
Dien Bien Phu
Dionysus
Disraeli
Djibouti
Dobermann pinscher
Dolgellau, Gwynedd
Domesday Book

Don Juan
Don Quixote
Doppelgänger
D'Oyly Carte Opera Company
Dungeness, Kent

Ebbw Vale, Gwent
Ecclesiastes
Ecumenical Council
Edinburgh
Eichmann Trial
Eisteddfod
Élysée Palace, France
Emmentaler cheese
Encyclopaedia Britannica
Entre-Deux-Mers
Eustachian tube
Evangelicalism
Excalibur
Existentialism
Ezekiel

Fabergé (jewelled eggs)
Faerie Queene, The
Feock, Cornwall
Fernet Branca
Fledermaus, Die (Strauss opera)
Folies-Bergère
Forsyte Saga
Führer, Der
Fu Manchu, Dr (Chinese movie detective)

Gallipoli
Gandhi
Gethsemane
Gewürztraminer
Gioconda, La (Mona Lisa)
Givenchy (fashion house)
Glyndebourne Festival

Gobelins tapestry
Godalming, Surrey
Gondoliers, The (Gilbert and Sullivan opera)
Goonhilly Downs
Gorgonzola
Götterdämmerung
Graf Zeppelin
Gruyère cheese
Guggenheim Museum, New York
Guinness
Gujarati
Gulbenkian Foundation
Gurkha

Habeas Corpus
Hallelujah Chorus
Hanukkah (sometimes Chanukkah)
Hawaiian
Heraklion, Crete
Herstmonceux, Sussex
Hippocratic Oath
Hiroshima
Houdini
Houyhnhnms (breed of horses in *Gulliver's Travels*)
Huguenots

Iago
Ightham, Kent
Immelmann turn
Indianapolis
Innisfail, Ireland
Inveraray Castle
Iolanthe (Gilbert and Sullivan opera)
Izvestia (Russian newspaper)

Jakarta, Indonesia
Jeroboam
Jodrell Bank
Juilliard School of Music, New York

Jungian psychology

Kafkaesque
Kama Sutra
Keynsian economic theories
Khartoum
Khmer Rouge
Kirkcudbright
Kirkintilloch
Kirriemuir
Knaresborough
Kubla Khan
Ku Klux Klan
Kyrie eleison

The Pitfalls of Word Recognition

Just as it's not uncommon to mistake a person for someone else, we can all fail to recognise words at times. Often, a single misplaced letter is all it takes to transform a simple statement into an unfortunate pun. Here is a small collection contributed by the public.

His record high jump was sheer poultry in motion.
It is true that no man is in Ireland.
He immediately flew into a high dungeon.
Unfortunately, his father died interstate.
I wouldn't touch it with a ten-foot Pole.
After the storm the beach was covered with jellyfish testicles.
A strange child, and old beyond her ears . . .

La donna è mobile (aria from *Rigoletto*)
La Guardia Airport, New York
Lalique glass
Lascaux Caves, France

Lausanne, Switzerland
Legionnaires' disease
Leicestershire
Leighton Buzzard
Leipzig
Lichtenstein
Liebfraumilch
Lilliputian
Lindbergh baby kidnapping
Lindisfarne, Holy Island off Northumberland coast
Linlithgow
Linnean Society
Llandrindod Wells, Powys
Llandudno, Gwynedd
Llanelli, Dyfed
Llangollen, Clwyd
Llareggub (the town in Dylan Thomas's *Under Milk
    Wood*)
Lohengrin
Looe, Cornwall
Louis Quinze
Lourdes, France
Lucia di Lammermoor
Luxembourg
Lyonnaise
Lysistrata (Aristophanes' comedy)

McCarthyism
Machiavellian
Machu Picchu, Peru
Magdalen College, Oxford
Magdalene College, Cambridge
Mahabharata (Hindu epic poem)
Mahatma Gandhi
Mahdi (Muslim messiah)
Maigret, Inspector
Maitre d'hôtel
Majolica (opaque glazed pottery)
Malagasy Republic (Madagascar)

Malawi (formerly Nyasaland)
Malthusianism
Mancunian

> **Lost Beauties** In 1874 the lexicographer Charles
> Mackay published *Lost Beauties of the English
> Language*, in which he bemoaned the fact that
> several thousand words in the language had fallen
> out of use. For bad spellers, this was good news,
> but on the other hand many of the lost words
> were colourfully expressive, as these few examples
> show:
>
> | benothinged | *annihilated* |
> | drouthy | *thirsty* |
> | jobbernowle | *thickhead* |
> | maw-wallop | *badly cooked* |
> | wowf | *bonkers* |
> | spousalbreach | *adultery* |
> | tapsalteerie | *topsyturvy* |
> | unbuxom | *scraggy* |
> | wanchancie | *unlucky* |
> | shoon | *plural of shoe* |

Manon Lescaut (novel and opera)
Manzanilla dry sherry
Mao Tse-tung, or Mao Zedong
Maraschino cherry
Marseillaise, The
Marylebone, London
Massachusetts
Mau Mau (Kenyan nationalist movement)
Meccano
Mediterranean
Meissen porcelain
Mennonite religion
Mephistopheles
Mesopotamia
Messerschmitt

Methuselah
Meursault, Burgundy white wine
Michaelmas
Milwaukee, Wisconsin, USA
Minneapolis, Minnesota, USA
Minotaur
Misérables, Les (Victor Hugo's 1862 novel)
Mississippi
Missolonghi, Greece
Missouri
Mistinguette (Paris music-hall star)
Mitsubishi
Möbius loop
Mogadishu, Somalia
Mohammed
Mohave Desert, USA
Mohican Indians
Monégasque (citizen of Monaco)
Montaigne, French essayist
Montessori teaching system
Montezuma
Montmartre, Paris
Montparnasse, Paris
Montreux Festival
Montserrat
Morocco
Morte d'Arthur
Moulin Rouge
Münchausen, Baron
Mustapha Kemal (Turkish leader)
Mycenaean civilisation

Narcissus
Nassau, Bermuda
Navaho Indian tribe
Neanderthal Man
Nebuchadnezzar
Nehru
Nefertiti (Egyptian queen)

Nietzsche, Friedrich
Nostradamus
Nouvelle cuisine
Nuneham Courtenay, Oxfordshire
Nürburgring (Grand Prix motor racing circuit,
    Germany)

Oberammergau, Bavaria
Odysseus
Odyssey, The (Homer's epic poem)
Oedipus complex
Oerlikon gun
Ombudsman
Oradour massacre, France
Orpheus and Eurydice
Orrefors glass (Swedish)
Oswestry, Shropshire
Oundle, Northamptonshire
Ozymandias (Shelley's sonnet)

Paleolithic Age
Paleozoic Era
Palladian architecture
Panmunjom, Korea
Paraguay, South America
Parisienne
Passchendaele (Belgian World War I battlefield)
Pathétique, The (Beethoven piano sonata)
Peloponnesian War
Pennsylvania
Pentateuch
Pepys's Diary
Phaethon
Philadelphia
Philippine Islands
Piccadilly Circus, London
Pierrot

Beware Welsh!

In the Principality of Wales there is still a considerable amount of Welsh spoken, and even more written. Names that English-speakers know and love – Brecon Beacons, Snowdonia, Cardiff and Holyhead, for example, can, on a signpost or a map, change in a flash to Bannau Brycheiniog, Eryri, Caerdydd and Caergybi respectively. The Welsh are always sympathetic to the vain efforts of outsiders trying to master the language, and you will earn extra kudos by being able to correctly spell at least a few of the names important to their history and culture. Try these:

> Cymru (Wales)
> Dewi Sant (St David, patron saint of Wales)
> Rhodri Fawr (ninth-century king who united Wales)
> Llywelyn the Great (King of Wales who died 1240)
> Dafydd ap Gwilym (famous Welsh poet, died fourteenth century)
> Owain Glyndŵr (creator of the first Welsh parliament)

Plaid Cymru (Welsh nationalist party)
Pleiades galaxy
Pleistocene
Portuguese
Poseidon
Poughkeepsie, New York
Presbyterian
Ptolemy
Pygmalion
Pyongyang, North Korea
Pyramus and Thisbe
64

Pyrenees
Pythagoras

Qaddafi, Muammar el–
Qantas
Qatar
Quattrocento
Quirinale, Rome

Rabelaisian
Ranunculus
Rashomon (classic 1951 Japanese movie)
Rastafarian
Rechabites (Friendly Society)
Reichstag
Renaissance
Reykjavik, Iceland
Rhesus (Rh) Factor
Rievaulx Abbey, Yorkshire
Riyadh, Saudi Arabia
Roget's Thesaurus
Roosevelt
Roquefort cheese and dressing
Rorschach Test
Rosencrantz and Guildenstern
Rosenkavalier, Der (Strauss opera)
Rosh Hashanah (Jewish New Year)
Rosicrucians
Rothschild
Rubáiyát of Omar Khayyám, The (Persian poem)
Rwanda

Sagittarius
Salzburg Festival
Sarajevo, Bosnia
Sartor Resartus
Saskatchewan, Canada
Savile Club, London
Saxmundham, Suffolk

Scheherazade
Schweppes
Scylla and Charybdis
Sequoia
Sèvres porcelain
Shepheard's Hotel, Cairo
Shoeburyness, Essex
Sicily
Siegfried
Sikhs
Sinai
Sinn Fein
Sioux Indians
Slivovitz (plum brandy)
Sohrab and Rustum

Grass Roots Spelling

Non-gardeners never fail to be perplexed, even
irritated, by the fluency with which the most
threatening botanical names trill from the tongues
of the professionals. They can spell them, too!
Here are some tricky ones you might like to sow
in your spell-check memory:

Agapanthus, Amaranthus, Amaryllis, Anemone,
Antirrhinum, Aquilegia, Aspidistra, Aubrietia,
Bignonia, Bougainvillea, Buddleia, Calycanthus,
Camellia, Ceanothus, Chrysanthemum,
Convolvulus, Cotoneaster, Cyananthus,
Cymbidium, Cytisus, Dahlia, Deutzia,
Dryopteris, Eucalyptus, Freesia, Fuchsia,
Gypsophila, Hyacinth, Impatiens, Liquidambar,
Narcissus, Nymphaea, Pelargonium,
Philodendron, Phlox, Pieris, Pyracantha,
Rhododendron, Stephanotis, Tradescantia,
Weigela, Yucca.

Sophocles
Sorbonne, The
Struwwelpeter (children's storybook character)
Sturm und Drang
Sudetenland
Sumer is icumen in
Sylphides, Les (ballet)

Taj Mahal
Tammany Hall
Tannhäuser (Wagner opera)
Tecumseh (Shawnee Indian chief)
Tennessee
Thermopylae
Tiffany
Tipperary, Ireland
Toynbee Hall, London
Transcendentalism
Trovatore, Il (Verdi opera)
Tschiffeley's Ride
Tutankhamen

Ulysses
Unter den Linden, Berlin
Utilitarianism

Valkyries
Velázquez
Venezuela
Versailles
Viet Minh
Vieux Carré, district of New Orleans
Vladivostok
Vlaminck, Maurice (French painter)

Wedgwood pottery
Wehrmacht
Welwyn, Hertfordshire
Wenceslas

Wickembreaux, Kent
Wilhelmstrasse, Berlin
Witwatersrand, South Africa
Woolf, Virginia
Wooloomooloo, New South Wales
Wootton Bassett, Wiltshire
Wroxeter, Shropshire
Wynken, Blynken and Nod

Xanadu (fabled city in Coleridge's poem, *Kubla Khan*)

Yangtze Kiang, China
Yom Kippur (Jewish Day of Atonement)
Yosemite, US national park

Zaire
Ziegfeld Girls
Zeppelin
Zimbabwe
Zinoviev Letter
Zoroastrianism

Spelling Test

The craft of spelling, as indicated earlier, is less a matter of rules and more a matter of remembering. Every word is different in some way, and many people do well by remembering these differences; simply by looking at a word they are able to tell if it looks 'right' or 'wrong'. If you have spent an hour browsing through this book, try this test. About half the words in this list are correct.

1. playright _____
2. accelerate _____
3. Luxembourg _____
4. biassed _____
5. diaphram _____
6. Portugese _____
7. repellent _____
8. surreptitious _____
9. suprintendent _____
10. Picadilly Circus _____
11. sizable _____
12. ricochet _____
13. permissable _____
14. conoisseur _____
15. Mitshibusi _____
16. fulsome _____
17. pavillion _____
18. personnel _____
19. titillation _____
20. neice _____

(*Answers over page*)

Answers to Spelling Test

1. playwright
2. correct
3. correct
4. biased
5. diaphragm
6. Portuguese
7. correct
8. correct
9. superintendent
10. Piccadilly Circus
11. correct
12. correct
13. permissible
14. connoisseur
15. Mitsubishi
16. correct
17. pavilion
18. correct
19. correct
20. niece

Scores: 20 correct – top of the class
15–18 – above average
14 – average
below 14 – browse for another hour and try again.

Good Grammar in One Hour

We all know more about grammar than we think.
Yet even the most learned authorities can't claim to
know it all. Written with the minimum of jargon,
Good Grammar in One Hour will allow you to polish
your native know-how, and to renew acquaintance
with the language and its working.

Crisp, Clear Writing in One Hour

Here are jargon and officialese hammered flat,
circumlocution and tautology brutally eliminated,
vogue words and verbiage sent packing. In just one
hour, a veteran Fleet Street sub-editor steers you
away from cliche, euphemism and muddle to leave
you with crisp, cogent, pared-down prose of which
you can be proud.

Word Bank
Expanding Your Vocabulary

The better you are at communicating, the more successful you are likely to be – and an effective vocabulary is the guarantee of clear, assured and persuasive speech and writing. *Word Bank* will expand your vocabulary and add force to your reasoning, conversation and self-confidence.

The Name Book

What's in a name? Here is everything you ever
needed to know about surnames, Christian names,
nicknames and odd names: what they mean, where
they came from and how they evolved. *The Name
Book* includes an insider's section on people who
have entered the language as words, a name-
dropper's list of those who have changed them and
an invaluable pronunciation guide.

Guide to Wordplay and Word Games

From acrostics and alternades to word-chains and word squares, and having fun with spoonerisms, clerihews, limericks, Scrabble and the crossword on the way, this book explores the wit and wonder of word games.

The Secrets of Speed Reading

How fast do you read? Reading faster not only enables you to absorb more material in any given time, but also improves comprehension and enhances enjoyment. With *The Secrets of Speed Reading*'s proven technique and sequence of instruction, exercises and self-tests, you can reach double, even triple, your present speeds for your own benefit and satisfaction – at home, at work, or even on holiday.

A Full List of Titles Available from Mandarin in this series

While every effort is made to keep prices low, it is sometimes necessary to increase prices at short notice. Mandarin Paperbacks reserves the right to show new retail prices on covers which may differ from those previously advertised in the text or elsewhere.

The prices shown below were correct at the time of going to press.

All these books are available at your bookshop or newsagent, or can be ordered direct from the publisher. Just tick the titles you want and fill in the form below.

Mandarin Paperbacks, Cash Sales Department, PO Box 11, Falmouth, Cornwall TR10 9EN.

Please send cheque or postal order, no currency, for purchase price quoted and allow the following for postage and packing:

UK including BFPO   £1.00 for the first book, 50p for the second and 30p for each additional book ordered to a maximum charge of £3.00.

Overseas including Eire   £2 for the first book, £1.00 for the second and 50p for each additional book thereafter.

NAME (Block letters) ....

ADDRESS ....

....

☐ I enclose my remittance for ....

☐ I wish to pay by Access/Visa Card Number

Expiry Date